Text and all photography: **GARY LADD** . Page, Arizona / canyonladd@page.az.net

Design, editing, production, and other stuff: **CAROL HARALSON** . Sedona, Arizona / carolharalson@esedona.net

A LADDSCAPES PRESS BOOK

P. O. BOX 2824 / 1908 RIM VIEW DRIVE, PAGE, ARIZONA 86040 / TEL. 928-645-3901

International Standard Book Number 0-9779318-0-3

Printed in China

What's The Hub?

PAGE THROUGH AND SEE!

 hotogenic

 stronomical

 eologic

 xact center

Escalante Canyon

The hub of the visual universe should, of course, be located on a thriving planet. It should be a place paved with naked rock rather than concrete, a place free of smothering vegetation, a place blessed with crystalline night views of the universe beyond Planet Earth. It should sit smack in the center of some of Earth's most fantastic landscapes.

This is Page.

From a photographic point of view, northern Arizona and southern Utah are indisputably The Hub. Look around: There's wild, wrinkled, convoluted, seductive terrain along every line of sight. Mysterious landforms inscribed with exotic, curving and linear patterns, cross-bedding, fracturing and erosion. Not even the wonders of the photographically and historically important Sierra Nevada are a match for the charms of canyon country in Utah and Arizona.

The Hub, however, is not really so much a physical location as a state of mind. The terrains here—from the controversial Lake Powell and lost Glen Canyon to the sublime Grand Canyon to the Paria Plateau with its swirling sandstones—all refresh the human psyche like a mid-July monsoon downpour refreshes the smoldering desert. Our environments profoundly influence us, our creativity, our moods, our well-being. Old familiar environments can become shopworn and dreary, lulling us to sleep; interesting new environments can snap us awake.

In the interest of full disclosure, however, it should be mentioned that The Hub does harbor a dark side. It is this: Page is a sacrifice area. The heartbreakingly charming landscape that lies beneath Lake Powell has been sacrificed to regulate the Colorado River, generate electricity and provide

WELCOME TO THE HUB

recreation for masses of people. The clean air above The Hub has been sacrificed to provide still more electricity, by the nearby Navajo Generating Station. Both of these projects were created to satisfy the country's burgeoning population and its insatiable appetites for more of everything.

Nevertheless, the Page-area landscapes are beyond compare. Consult the local place names for clues to their appeal: Rainbow Bridge, Point Sublime, Echo Cliffs, The Wave, Quite-a-Mess, the Corkscrew, Elves Chasm, Forest Alcove, The Big Cut, Blue Moon Bench, Maureen's Ravine, Forbidding Canyon, Area 52 and Skip's Decoy. At these wonderful places and hundreds more, visitors can look down by day and examine the bare bones of Planet Earth; can look up by night to the bare bones of deep space and the faint glow of the Andromeda Galaxy.

More than any former human generation, ours understands the histories of the fundamental features of our universe—the stars, the galaxies, the Moon, our own Earth's rocks, oceans and life. It's a privilege to possess these treasures of knowledge. It is, in fact, a miracle. Those who live at or visit The Hub can connect with and appreciate our place in the cosmos as no other humans have before.

Welcome to The Hub of the Visual Universe, Page, Arizona.

GARY LADD
Official Copy Serial Number 6231

Ⓟ Ⓐ Ⓖ Ⓔ 5

6 quick tips for visitors to The Hub

1 If you find that you can't resist carving your name or initials in the rocks of the Colorado Plateau, be sure you send your full name and address to the administering agency (National Park Service or Bureau of Land Management) for official recognition. (Then, make plans for an extended all-expenses-paid return visit to The Hub.)

2 The fabled carcass-fancying California condor has been reintroduced into The Hub. Never feed a condor; don't approach one. (And, for sure, don't look as if you are dead.)

3 Rattlesnakes are sometimes encountered in The Hub. Really, don't worry your head one little bit. But somewhere in the back of your mind, keep a stay-alert-to-coiled-or-sinuous shapes program running. Most importantly, if you do come upon a rattlesnake, do not tease it or mess with it. (Special note to all visiting macho guys: The courageous are snakebit far more often than the meek.)

4 If it is summer, roaring hot, and you're out in the sun, drink plenty of water. Beer and soda do nothing to keep you hydrated. Headaches, grumpiness and nausea are common signs of dehydration (and pregnancy).

5 Play smart around The Hub. The Hub's landscapes are wonder-filled and irresistible. But they are also unfamiliar to most visitors. It is surprisingly easy to do incredibly dumb

things in this unusual environment where common sense has had little or no chance to develop. Think twice about every activity—boating, swimming, hiking, climbing, drinking alcohol. Little mistakes in an unfamiliar environment can be surprisingly lethal. Be particularly careful on the rim of Grand Canyon. (Especially when there's a condor around looking hopeful.)

6 Don't worry about quicksand. In canyons with wet, sandy floors, a person can occasionally sink in quicksand to knee or thigh level. It is an inconvenience and you can lose your shoe, but the local quicksand will not swallow you whole. To get out, enlist the help of others or just lie down on the surface and slowly extricate your legs. Crawl to stable ground. This may take a few minutes but you'll get out. (Just hope a rattlesnake doesn't come by.)

Page and the Lake Powell area:

FAQ*s and iFAQ**s

*Frequently asked questions

**Infrequently asked questions

1 **How did Page get its name?** Until 1957 the site of Page was part of the Navajo Nation. Shortly after work began on Glen Canyon Dam, Manson Mesa was obtained in a land trade. The new town on the mesa above the dam was named after John C. Page, a former commissioner of the Bureau of Reclamation. The city is still trying to recover from its orchestrated government birth. Its physical layout, its lack of home mail delivery, and its general dysfunctional quirkiness are all traceable to the federal government's original good intentions. The city of Page covers about 17 square miles surrounded by the Navajo Indian Reservation and Glen Canyon National Recreation Area.

Note: Manhattan Island (also obtained in trade from Native Americans) at 23 square miles, is about 50 percent larger than Page. If Page had the population density of Manhattan, 1 million people would live here, a truly terrifying concept.

2 **Why are the churches of Page lined up in a row along the main drag?** The federal government's Bureau of Reclamation planned the city of Page to be compact and orderly. Specific areas were designated for businesses, schools and residential neighborhoods. Because the influence of religion was seen as an important stabilizing factor in an otherwise restless construction camp, the Bureau offered to any religious denomination a free plot of land. The plots were located side by side, prominently, on the city's principal boulevard, to eventually become known as Church Row.

Reflection Canyon, lake down 140 feet from full.

3 Why was the Navajo Generating Station built here in such an otherwise visually pristine landscape, especially when Glen Canyon Dam already generates so much electricity? In the 1960s a consortium of power companies and the Bureau of Reclamation proposed a hydroelectric dam in Grand Canyon's Marble Gorge. When Congress denied authorization for this dam in the upper reaches of Grand Canyon, the consortium re-submitted, but replaced the proposed dam with a coal-fired power plant 50 miles northeast of the dam site. This plan was approved by government agencies. With an output of 2,250 megawatts, nearly twice that of Glen Canyon Dam, the Navajo Generating Station is the largest coal-fired power plant west of the Mississippi River. It was dedicated in 1976. The white clouds rising from the three 775-foot high smokestacks are composed mostly of steam, not smoke. Sometimes on calm days a reddish-brown sky smudge appears in the vicinity of the plant. This is a photochemical smog, mostly nitrogen oxides, a pollution that escapes the generating station's considerable environmental protection systems.

4 What is the summit elevation of Navajo Mountain (the mountain on the eastern horizon about 35 miles away)? 10,388 feet (about 6,700 feet above a full Lake Powell). For comparison, the San Francisco Peaks north of Flagstaff rise to 12,633 feet. Geologists call Navajo Mountain a *laccolithic* mountain, one that was formed by the intrusion of *magma* (molten rock) into sedimentary layers of the upper crust forcing the overlying surface rock to bulge upwards. Navajo Mountain has the heart of a volcano, a countenance of serenity.

Dam!

Aerial: Labyrinth Canyon

Aerial: Boaters at camp near Padre Bay

Aerial: Mouth of Face Canyon

5 When was Glen Canyon Dam built and how does it compare to Hoover Dam? Construction of Glen Canyon Dam began in 1956. It was completed in 1963. Hoover Dam, completed in 1935, rises 726 feet from bedrock, 16 feet higher than Glen Canyon Dam. Hoover Dam is also about twice as thick as Glen Canyon Dam. But because Glen Canyon is considerably wider than Black Canyon at the Hoover Dam site, the volume of concrete used in each project was similar, about 5 million cubic yards. Glen Canyon Dam's Lake Powell is longer than Hoover Dam's Lake Mead but Lake Powell's volume is slightly less than Lake Mead's.

6 Are those small, gray, lumpy hills along US 89 between Page and Cameron tailings piles created by mining activities? No, they are not. The hills are completely natural exposures of Chinle Shale, the same rock unit that contains most of the petrified wood in Petrified Forest National Park and the Lees Ferry area.

7 Are the cliffs that surround Page the result of upheavals along fault lines? No, they are not. These cliffs are the slowly receding faces of layer upon layer of rock being slowly dismantled by time, weathering, and erosion. The cliffs are the edges of once more-widespread sheets of rock that have so far survived eons of exposure to the surface environment. (Remember that rock units spend most of their lifetimes buried far beneath the surface by other, younger rock units. By the time we see them on the surface, they are near the end of their lives, in the process, or soon to be in the process, of being dismantled and swept away.) The cliffs continue to weather slowly, gradually receding from the Colorado River and its tributaries as they fall victim to rain, freezing temperatures, biologic forces and the inexorable tug of gravity. Sporadic rainfalls transport fallen particles and pieces of the disintegrating cliffs downhill into the washes and canyons that eventually take them to the Colorado River. The cliff lines tend to parallel drainage channels, even when those drainages are almost always dry.

8 Who are the Native Americans commonly seen in Page? Most are Navajos. The Navajo Indian Reservation borders the southern and eastern boundaries of Page. The Navajos probably arrived in The Hub about 1500 AD, close to the time Christopher Columbus arrived on the eastern edge of North America.

9 Why do I sometimes see pickup trucks hauling large plastic or metal tanks in their beds? Most likely the tanks are for transporting water. Many hogans (traditional Navajo homes) have no running water. Domestic water must be trucked to them.

10 How big is Lake Powell and how soon will it fill with silt? When it is full, Lake Powell holds about two years' flow of the Colorado River, about eight cubic miles of water. Because of commitments to downstream users, 17 years were required to fill the lake. Climate change and human activities in the watershed could easily skew the numbers, but the Bureau of Reclamation predicts that silt will fill Lake Powell in about 700 years.

Ice Cream Scoop Rock

11 When were the slot canyons discovered? The Native Americans have known about the slot canyons for generations. But in a land sprinkled with wonders, slot canyons were of no particular interest to the natives. When Page was founded and thousands of outsiders arrived, Antelope Canyon became a local hangout and curiosity. No one foresaw, even as late as the early 1980s, that the canyon would become internationally famous.

12 Why is this area sooo unusually scenic? It's The Hub's uncommon geologic history. Like all of the Colorado Plateau, the Page area features a thick sequence of flat-lying rock units, most of them sedimentary and representing tens and hundreds of millions of years of geologic history. Most importantly, the thick sequence of rock was then uplifted thousands of feet by tectonic plate movements and then carved profoundly by a large river that gathers its waters from the distant Rocky Mountains. Finally, because the area is a desert, very little vegetation obscures the scenic landforms.

13 Where are the trails in the Lake Powell area? There aren't any. Well, there aren't very many. This area was developed after trails fell into disfavor. And, truthfully, there's little need for them. The Lake Powell area is not nearly as rugged as Grand Canyon. A topographic map, a talent for route-finding, a thirst for exploration and an understanding of how some routes just don't work is all that's needed. However, high summer temperatures, lack of water, and deceptive distances make foot travel hazardous to those unfamiliar with the area. Trails make overland travel easier; route-finding makes overland travel interesting.

14 Where did all this sand come from? The sand around Lake Powell, on the Paria Plateau, around Page and on the Navajo Indian Reservation comes primarily from weathered Navajo Sandstone. Because the Navajo Sandstone underlies much of the local terrain and because it is over 1,000 feet thick in the Page area, there's ample Navajo Sandstone influence on the local landscape. The Navajo Sandstone weathers into quartz grains, the sand that mantles so much of The Hub.

15 Why does Page have so many schools? The Page public school system is remarkably large for a city of about 8,000 inhabitants because over half of the students, about 1,700 of them, are bussed into town from surrounding remote areas. The school district covers 2,400 square miles—twice the area of Rhode Island!—sometimes requiring an hour-long bus ride twice each school day. Seventy-three percent of the students in the Page schools are Native American.

16 Why are stupid, dirty, pie-plopping, methane-spewing cows allowed to trample Anasazi Indian ruins, crush fragile soils, foul springs and despoil photographically priceless slickrock areas? Believe it or not, in spite of their rather poor scholarly record, cows have tenure. And (by way of their owners) they have the ear of Congress. Personally, I am utterly disgusted by the situation. My solution: When hoofing it across scenic public lands used for grazing, I sometimes wear a cow suit that confers upon me a legitimacy and respect greater than that accorded to me as a mere H. *sapiens*. And, as my friends are happy to point out, the disguise also improves my appearance.

Azar (who else?)

17 Are those large, black, noisy birds that hang around Lake Powell beaches and Grand Canyon river camps called crows? Nope, they are ravens, larger cousins of the crows. Ravens are extremely intelligent. They can open zippers, rummage through the beds of grocery-laden pickup trucks, fly upside down, and carry away unattended platter-sized, delicious, juicy steaks. They're amusing, amazing, cute and entertaining unless it was your steak that just flew across the river.

18 What is that white ring around the edge of Lake Powell? The so-called "bathtub ring" shows the level of Lake Powell when it's full. It's not a bleaching of the rock but a coating composed mostly of calcium carbonate (precipitated out of the water) and dead plant material. When the lake goes down the bathtub ring begins to degrade. In some places it peels off quite readily, in others where the underlying rock is more stable, it will likely last for centuries. I like to call the band of terrain between the current lake level and former high lake levels the Zone of Wretchification.

19 Is it true that Page has a wicked reputation in some circles? Indeed! The flooding of Glen Canyon, the alteration of the river environment in Grand Canyon, the extraction of coal and the degradation of air quality associated with the Navajo Generating Station are all distressing, no argument there. On the other hand, all of us vote for such projects every time we flip on the air conditioning, water the lawn or eat an artichoke trucked from California's Imperial Valley. Places like Page are handy targets, but only part of a complex problem that involves us all, and the choices we make.

20 Should we be concerned about global warming and world climate change? Very.

20 ANSWERS:
What to do at The Hub

1) Tour Glen Canyon Dam and Carl Hayden Visitor Center
2) Catch a Lake Powell tour boat to Rainbow Bridge
3) Hike to Horseshoe Bend (Tad Nichols Overlook)
4) Visit the John Wesley Powell Museum
5) Rent a Lake Powell houseboat, speedboat or kayak for a day or a week
6) Take a day trip to Grand Canyon's North Rim
7) Visit Lees Ferry and the Lonely Dell Historic District
8) Walk across the Colorado River on historic Navajo Bridge and watch for California condors
9) Go swimming in Lake Powell
10) Visit Antelope Canyon Navajo Tribal Park
11) Explore the Grand Staircase–Escalante National Monument
12) Drive to Grand Canyon's South Rim for the day
13) Take a half-day flatwater float trip on the Colorado River from Glen Canyon Dam to Lees Ferry
14) Go hiking or backpacking in Vermilion Cliffs National Monument
15) Make a road trip to Navajo National Monument and Monument Valley Navajo Tribal Park
16) Go fishing on the Colorado River upstream from Lees Ferry
17) Get in an airplane to see the extraordinary local topography from above it all
18) Walk or mountain bike Page's Rim Trail
19) Take time to write to your congressman or woman about any of dozens of disastrous federal debacles
20) Play golf on the Lake Powell National Golf Course
21) *(Bonus answer):* Sit down, rest and relax

 19

hotogenic

astronomical

geologic

exact center

Too photogenic to be true

Bad news, friends. An army has invaded The Hub. The invaders are grimly determined and heavily armed photographers.

I'm not particularly fond of photographers. They often gather into packs (called "workshops"), they converse in an arcane language ("f16 @ 1/125th") and, quite frankly, are sometimes too single-minded in their dogged pursuit of some photographic objective (sometimes getting out of bed at 1:30 a.m.). Even worse, rather than search out new photogenic locations or opportunities, many photographers expend their energy on the reconstruction of images previously captured by other photographers. (To one degree or another, all photographers do this—it's one way in which we learn.) But the overzealous pursuit of replication can be stupid and self-defeating.

There's good reason for the photographer hordes to descend on this part of the world: The terrain is almost too photogenic to be true. The slickrock and canyon terrain that surrounds The Hub has displaced the Sierra Nevada as the touchstone of landscape photography in the western U.S.

A terrain almost too good to be true is, in fact, a bit of a problem. Everyone, photographers included, is impressed and moved by the local scenery, especially The Hub's large-scale scenery. The contours of Coyote Buttes, the rim views of Grand Canyon, the wide expanses Lake Powell's Padre Bay are nearly irresistible. But the finest images (those that while as striking as the old proven standbys, are refreshingly unique and creative) often hide in the details of a larger scene—in the foregrounds, in the close-ups and in the near-at-hand.

For photographers there is much to know and much to value in the landscapes of The Hub of the Visual Universe: There are its details, its topography, the nature of the light that falls upon them, its weather and much more than can be covered here. Nevertheless, here are some thoughts about photographing The Hub.

Grand Canyon, river mile 53

Clockwise from left: Escalante side canyon,
Porcupine at lunch, Ephemeral waterfall
during a November downpour

Generally, for better images
of the Colorado Plateau

> **Remember that superior images are a direct result of the amount of effort invested.**

Carrying and using a tripod is a headache. But tripods are often essential for making sharp images (especially while working in low light or when using long lenses). Climbing a hill or scaling a cliff to get a better angle is a pain but it can make a better image. Being patient is an annoyance but it sometimes pays big dividends. All of these things are work, but they are also effective techniques for improving one's chances of coming home with high quality images.

Good photography usually requires more work—there's just no way around it.

> **Remember to, in one way or another, move in close.**

By "move in close" I mean fill the frame with the best the scene has to offer. Physically, move in close to eliminate distracting elements. Optically, move in close with a telephoto or zoom lens. Move in close with a wide angle to include both a foreground and distant elements. Move in close with a close-up lens to show the beauty of the small. Move in close with a wide angle lens to include more of a striking pattern or to emphasize dramatic curving or sweeping lines. One way or another, photographers should remember to move in close to strengthen the scene's composition.

Gunsight Butte and Navajo Mountain, Prickly-pear

Most subjects require flattering light.

The illumination of a distant subject, a mesa that stands a mile or two away for instance, is not very forgiving. Distance exaggerates the blues and subdues the reds. It also allows almost no way to select the quality of light—the subject is too far away to easily change your relation to it. The only effective way you can change it is by waiting for the light itself to change, by waiting for the sun to move or for clouds to roll in or out.

With nearby subjects, however, you can change the illumination not only by waiting but by viewing another side of the subject, or by simply selecting a subject that's currently flattered by its illumination. I look for subjects that are, right now, illuminated by warm, diffuse light reflected from a nearby cliff. I look for subjects that lend themselves to backlighting and that, right now, are in fact backlit. I look for horizontal foregrounds that are pleasingly illuminated by the blue sky above while the mid-distance, in contrast, is illuminated by orange light reflecting from a cliff.

If your intention is to create an artistic landscape image, look for subjects and compositions that possess compelling patterns, symmetries and broken symmetries. Look for diverging lines (as with the leaves of an agave plant), parallel lines (as with a grove of ponderosa pine trees), circles and arcs (as with natural bridges and arches), sweeping or curving lines (as with the bedding patterns in Navajo Sandstone).

A photo possessing a strong basic geometric structure is often also an intriguing photo.

Sky pool, Forest Alcove

Reflections, Escalante Canyon, Facing page: Aerial: Padres Butte

> **Remember the power of a human figure within the grand drama of the landscape.**

Including a person in a landscape scene can add just the right amount of focus, color, interest and scale. This sounds easy but can be tricky. Use care in the following:

Place the person where he or she is most pleasingly illuminated.

Place the person against an uncluttered background.

Place the person at the best distance for maximum impact (nearby or far away).

Place the person in the frame where most effective (near the center or closer to the periphery).

Finally, it's usually best to photograph the person looking toward the scene's center.

> **To be an honest-to-goodness *good* photographer you must seek out new images.**

You must not merely successfully copy the pleasing images of others. Little else is as satisfying as the capture and publication of an image that other photographers have overlooked.

Sacred datura; Rainbow Bridge

Narrow-leaf yucca amid manzanita

Specifically, for better images
in Antelope Canyon

Photography in Antelope Canyon is inspiring, frustrating, rewarding and surprisingly time-consuming. You'll likely use your camera and its controls as never before so be prepared to both discover overlooked capabilities and annoying deficiencies in your system. One reminder—turn off your image stabilization system when using a tripod.

Review your camera's instruction manual before entering the canyon. Review how to enable or disable the following camera features: aperture-priority, time exposures, auto-bracketing, auto-focus, and automatic flash. It's smart to take your instruction manual with you even though once in the canyon it's often awkward and inefficient to figure out how to operate unfamiliar camera features.

A photography session in Upper Antelope Canyon is physically easy—its floor is mostly flat and sandy. A trip through Lower Antelope Canyon, however, requires a climb up and down a series of metal stairways bolted to the walls. It also requires some ducking, careful footwork, grunting and upper body maneuvering. Unless you've explored a tight slot canyon before, you can't possibly imagine what hiking through the canyon's many wiggles and twists can entail. Carrying a tripod and camera through the convolutions of Lower Antelope is therefore a bit of a challenge. Make sure you don't bang your camera into a canyon wall as you watch your footwork on the metal steps or mind your elbows and head while in the midst of an otherwise beautifully fluid and well-executed "Navajo reverse oblique double thrust traverse" in any of the canyon's many multilateral contortions.

Both Upper and Lower Antelope are short, less than a quarter mile long in both cases. Many visitors to Lower Antelope Canyon, however, because of its various contortive challenges, estimate its length at close to a mile.

ABCs of photographing
Antelope Canyon

A PERTURE: Most images of the canyon require substantial depth of focus (sometimes called depth of field). Be sure to use smaller apertures (larger numbers on the aperture scale) to obtain greater depth of focus. You may find it convenient to use your camera in aperture-priority mode. Note that small apertures yield long exposure times, making necessary the use of a tripod.

B LUE SKY ILLUMINATION: Many of the most pleasing Antelope Canyon images include not only the warm glow of sunlight reflecting from a hidden wall onto a visible wall but also sections of canyon wall illuminated primarily by the faint radiance of the blue sky. This faint blue sky illumination is subtle and difficult to sense with the unaided eye. Your camera, however, will record it. The combination of cool blue sky light illumination and warm orange reflected sunlight illumination can be extremely appealing.

B RACKETING: The atmosphere in Antelope is so unworldly that standard exposure is often not the most effective or pleasing exposure. Try bracketing, that is, expose one frame at the meter's recommended settings, another frame underexposed about 2/3 stop and a third frame overexposed about 2/3 stop. Digital photographers will be able to review their images to see what works best.

C ROWDS: In the warmer months, be prepared for a canyon jammed with tourists. For this reason, photographs that include the lower canyon walls are often difficult. Be prepared to lose photographs when someone walks into your scene during a time exposure. Stay calm! Never rant! Be prepared to wait while others complete their time exposure photographs.

D UST AND SAND: Dust and sand are nasty problems when the canyon is full of people shuffling through or when it's windy. Any time you change film or change

lenses airborne grit can get into your camera. For digital cameras this means dust on your sensor; for film cameras this means scratched film or worse. If sand is drifting down into the canyon, do not change film or lenses. Even on calm days, minimize the number of times the camera is opened, have someone hover over you like an umbrella when you open your camera, or leave the canyon floor to change film or lenses. On windy days, dust and sand will accumulate on your lens if you are shooting upwards towards the sky. Occasionally blow off such sand and grit to avoid degraded images.

E XTRA EQUIPMENT: Take and use a tripod and a small flashlight. The canyon is very dark in some sections, especially early and late in the day, and especially in Upper Antelope. Depending upon the sensitivity of your film, exposure times in the range of 5 to 20 seconds are common. It is best to use a cable release, a remote release or the camera's self-timer to begin the exposure. A lens brush is a good idea, too.

 **F** LASH FLOOD DANGER: *Important—do not enter the canyon if it is threatening to rain anywhere in Antelope Canyon's drainage area.* Antelope Canyon funnels water from 15 to 20 miles to the south towards Lake Powell. You can drown in a flash flood initiated by a rainfall miles away.

H OT SPOT CAUTION: Images that include sections of canyon wall directly illuminated by the sun are often rendered as unpleasantly overexposed. Most of the time, you should try to eliminate or minimize such "hot spots" in your photographs. If you do include them, attempt to keep them small in size and of a pleasing shape. (The shape of the overexposed area, as recorded on film or on a digital sensor, will be extremely conspicuous.)

L ENS SELECTION: Most Antelope Canyon photographic possibilities call for medium to strong wide angle through medium telephoto lenses. In 35 mm format, this usually means 20 to 125 mm focal lengths.

ON-CAMERA FLASH: If you are using a tripod, for most photographs, do not use an on-camera flash. You'll usually do better by using the dim but dramatic natural light.

SUNBEAMS: In the dim light of the inner canyons, sunlight itself becomes a photogenic presence when there is dust in the air. Don't miss an opportunity to capture these spectacular beams with your camera. *Note: A person standing in such a beam of direct sunlight will often be recorded as a dazzling white "ghost" complete with a supernatural glow, looking less like a friend from home than a spirit from beyond the veil.* Sunbeams are most common in summer. Some photographers throw handfuls of sand into the air to brighten the beams. This technique can be very successful but it also tends to wreak havoc on cameras, film and CCD sensors. And it can discourage the goodwill of other canyon visitors.

SKY CONDITIONS: Clear skies are best. Cloudy skies produce a more even illumination in wider canyon sections but the resulting images are usually not as dramatic.

TIME OF DAY: Two to three hours before and after noon offer the greatest number of successful images but all times of the day offer some opportunities.

TIME OF YEAR: In general, summer is considered the best season for photography. However, summer brings crowds and the crowds can make serious photography almost impossible, especially if you are using a tripod. All seasons of the year are photographically rewarding if the sky is clear and the sun is shining. In the summer, both Antelope Canyon segments are a few degrees cooler than the surrounding sun-drenched desert. In mid-winter they can be cold, especially if it's breezy.

Modern convenience, Antelope Canyon

Double Visions

The lines and contours
of the local landscapes
often lend themselves to
creative interpretation.
Simply placing reversed
and normal images
side-by-side can create
imaginary but intriguing
worlds.

Double Vision I: Seeps spilling down Navajo Sandstone, Glen Canyon

Pages 36-37: Double Vision II: Cross-bedding

Pool and reflection

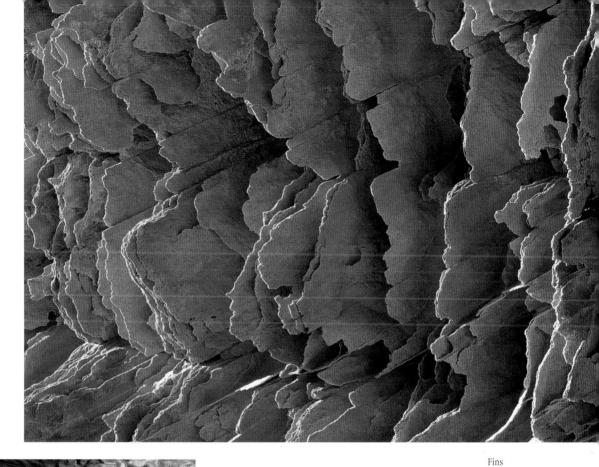

Fins

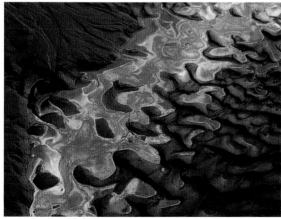

Ferruginous water

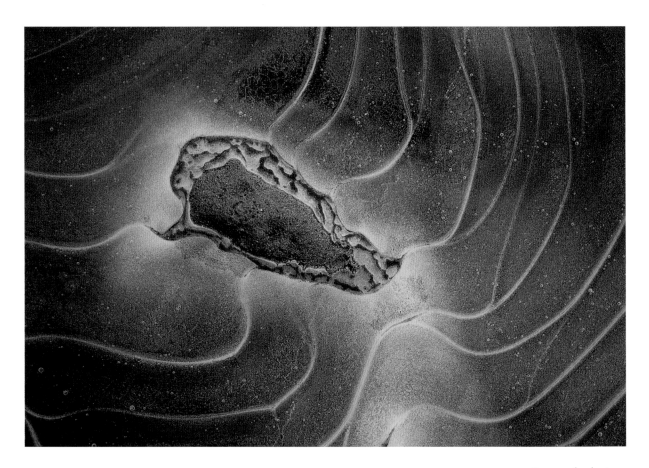

Frozen sand and water

Water and stone

Double Vision III: Colorado
River downstream of the dam

 43

Escalante Canyon tributary

Pool Canyon

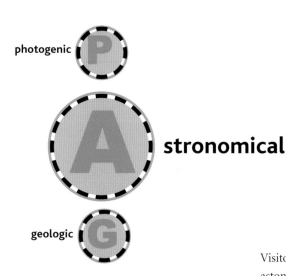

photogenic **P**

A stronomical

geologic **G**

exact center **E**

The Hub's dark sky

The sky above The Hub is largely unspoiled by manmade light pollution. Visitors to The Hub, especially those who come from glittering cities, may be as astonished by the night sky as they are by the landscape below it. It may be the first time they've had a sporting chance to follow the glow of the Milky Way from one horizon to another.

After Isaac Newton formulated his Universal Theory of Gravitation, the universe was assumed to be infinitely old and infinitely large. If it were otherwise gravity would draw all its contents—stars, planets, asteroids, comets and gases—together into a cataclysmic cosmic collision. Yet, there was no evidence of such contraction. The solution, therefore, was a universe in equilibrium by way of infinite size.

There was, however, an irritating problem with this concept. If the universe were infinite in size, then every line of sight from Earth into space should eventually fall upon the surface of a star. And if this were true, then the night sky should blaze as brightly as the surface of the sun. But it doesn't. This problem, Olber's Paradox, was a clue that the universe was neither infinite in age nor in size.

The astronomical study of the history and structure of the universe is called cosmology. (Careful, reader: This term should not be confused with the entirely different pursuit known as cosmetology.) From The Hub, cosmology is more accessible and more appropriate than from most earthly locations.

About 6,000 stars are bright enough to be detected by the naked eye. About 2,000 of them are visible at any one time under dark conditions. Across this field of sparkling heavenly diamonds wander the planets, the moon, shooting stars and the

Tower Butte and moonrise

occasional stray comet come to warm itself near the nuclear fires of the sun. The night sky is both ever-changing and never-changing. Here, at The Hub, the night sky will often exact its toll in sleep whenever an observer, lying on the rock and sand of the Colorado Plateau, merely looks up, away from the earth beneath.

In the late summer, the Andromeda Galaxy can be seen arcing up from the eastern horizon. This is the first object that Edwin Hubble, in 1924, found beyond our own Milky Way Galaxy. The discovery opened the door to the realization that with large telescopes equipped with high-efficiency detectors we Earthlings can see not only deep into space but far back into time because, in comparison to the titanic scale of inter-galactic distances, light travels at a snail's pace. And because intergalactic distances are so vast, by looking deep into space we are seeing objects as they were up to billions of years ago. The Andromeda Galaxy, for instance, lies 2.3 million light-years away. Look up at Andromeda tonight and you will see it as it was on an evening 2.3 million years ago.

The discovery of a galaxy beyond our own (an "island universe" in the parlance of the 1920s) soon led to Hubble's discovery of the expansion of the universe, a completely dumfounding revelation. With this, Einstein was forced to modify his general relativity equations. It all started with observations of the Andromeda Galaxy from southern California, but accessible to the naked eye from here at The Hub.

The sky teems with stars on moonless nights. And yet our eyes are just too small (that is, they possess apertures inadequate to bring enough photons to a focus on the retina) to detect the faint glow of anything but the closest and brightest of them.

Evening primrose

The human eye can detect bright stars flaming away at distances of perhaps 2,000 to 3,000 light-years. But our own home galaxy alone measures some 100,000 light-years across. We can't see, with our unaided eyes, many of the masses of neighboring stars. It is only the aggregate light of the perhaps 400 billion to a trillion stars within the Andromeda Galaxy that allows us to see it at a distance of millions of light-years.

Examine the sky with the appropriate instruments, interpret the data carefully and you will likely come to the following conclusions: Our universe was born in a "Big Bang" about 13.7 billion years ago when literally everything—space, mass, energy, even time— were born. (The name "Big Bang" was coined by Sir Fred Hoyle, an astronomer and staunch detractor of the theory. His term of derision somehow lodged in the astronomical psyche and pop culture, displacing other more dignified terms.) Big Bang theory tells us that only the lightest, simplest elements—hydrogen, helium and (a pinch of) lithium formed from more elementary particles. All other elements have since been cooked up in the interiors of stars as they've converted mass to energy, or (in the case of the heaviest elements) in the supernova death throes of the very largest stars. This means that most of the elements of which we are made and with which we are familiar were created in the cores of stars that lived and died billions of years ago, before our sun and our solar system were born.

The visible universe probably contains over 100 billion galaxies. The average galaxy contains about 100 billion stars. Out there, in a very alien, very harsh environment that we can hardly comprehend, stars are still being born and are still flaming out. Surprisingly, the biggest stars burn themselves to cinders the fastest (let that be a lesson to you!) in as little as 10 million years. The smallest stars smolder dimly and quietly for hundreds of billions of years.

Earth, born about the same time as our Sun, is 4.6 billion years old. Our planet has benefited from the work of previous generations of stars that cooked up heavier elements and later exploded, salting their neighborhoods with hoards of heavier elements such as oxygen, calcium, and iron. The clouds of debris from the explosions mingled with other interstellar atoms to eventually coalesce into new stars. Judging from the Sun's relative abundances of elements it is believed that it's a third-generation star.

The sun, as it ages, grows slowly brighter. In about 500 million to 1 billion years—a relatively short time even on the timescale of Earth's history—the sun will have grown bright enough to bring about the evaporation of Earth's oceans. By then, or shortly thereafter, nearly all life on Earth will perish. Ultimately the sun will flame out about 5 billion years from now.

Despite our best efforts, we still may not know much about the universe. We do not know, for instance, where most of its mass is hidden. We do not know much about what makes it expand at a rate that seems to be increasing. We do not know what lit the match of the Big Bang in the first place. And we do not know if there were or still are other universes that will forever lie beyond our ability to detect.

Look up into the sky and you'll find yourself drawn into the beauty and mystery of the nearly endless volumes of space that encapsulate The Hub.

Kane Point

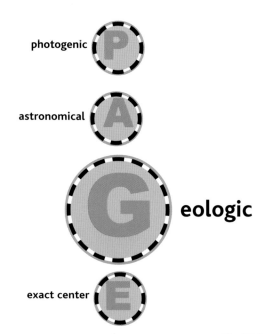

photogenic **P**

astronomical **A**

Geologic

exact center **E**

The geologic Hub

The Hub lies near the center of the Colorado Plateau.

What is the Colorado Plateau? It's an area about equal to the size of France that includes most of northern Arizona, the southeast half of Utah, and the corners of both southwestern Colorado and northwestern New Mexico. Monument Valley sits near the plateau's center.

What makes the Colorado Plateau unique? The Colorado Plateau is a geologic province lying between the Rocky Mountains to the east and north and the Basin and Range to the west and south. These surrounding regions are mountainous with rock units warped or tilted by mountain-building processes. In comparison, the rock units of the Colorado Plateau normally lie flat even though they too, like the mountains, have been pushed upwards thousands of feet by plate tectonic movements. In other words, the rock layers of the Colorado Plateau (which were originally laid down in horizontal sheets) remain relatively flat despite their large upwards displacement. Today these rock units are being exposed by the erosive power of the Colorado River and its tributaries.

Navajo Sandstone, 190 million years old
Facing page: Vishnu Group, 1.7 billion
years old

What's special about the Colorado River? The Colorado River, although not extremely impressive in volume, possesses an unusually steep gradient. In Grand Canyon the Colorado River drops nearly eight feet in elevation per river mile. In comparison, the Mississippi drops about six inches per mile. It is the Colorado's inherent steepness that multiplies its erosional power and its ability to carve deep the canyons. Although the Mississippi River carries about 30 times the volume of the Colorado River, its low gradient restricts its ability to carry sediment to less than twice the Colorado's. In other words, the Colorado River is 17 times muddier than the muddy Mississippi. Particle by particle, the Colorado River is rapidly hauling away the rock of the mountains and plateaus to the Gulf of California.

The voracious river has exposed dozens of ancient rock units, each expressing its personality . . .

The voracious river has exposed dozens of ancient rock units, each expressing its personality via color, texture, fossil assemblage and its propensity to make one or another unusual landscape feature—arches, water pockets, balanced rocks, cliffs, domes, bridges, slot canyons, plateaus, buttes, and more.

The Colorado Plateau is a great outdoor museum of geology with an extensive collection (its many rock units), a simple and effective display system (uplift by plate movements and the subsequent carving by the Colorado River) and an excellent environmental control system (low rainfall and the resultant lack of vegetation).

How old are the local rocks? Unlike the canyons (which are recent developments) the rocks of The Hub are relatively old. In the area of The Hub the rocks are almost all *sedimentary* (rock first laid down as deposits in low-lying areas) rather than *igneous* (rock emplaced in a molten state such as by volcanoes) or *metamorphic* (rock modified by heat and pressure by having been once buried especially far below the surface as in the case with the Vishnu Group rocks in the bottom of the Grand Canyon).

Because the rock units have been left largely undisturbed by faulting and folding, the youngest rocks still lie on top, (Bryce Canyon's Claron Formation, for instance, dates to about 50 million years ago) and the oldest rocks still lie at the bottom (the Grand Canyon's Vishnu Group are up to 1,840 million years old.) Glen Canyon rocks are roughly 200 million years old. For comparison, the age of the Earth comes to about 4,600 million years while the canyons themselves (the excavations made by the Colorado River) are believed to be only 5 or 6 million years old.

Slot Canyon and wedged boulders

Cracked silt beds as Lake Powell recedes

When and how far was the Colorado Plateau uplifted? The Colorado Plateau began to gain elevation about 70 million years ago. Since then there has been little opportunity for the deposition of sand, silt and mud that could harden into sedimentary rock. (The deposition of material destined to become sedimentary rock usually occurs in low-lying areas such as ocean basins, swamps, river deltas, shoreline sand dunes, lake beds, etc. where water and wind have carried it from surrounding higher terrains.) Erosion—the removal of material from terrains exposed to the effects of water, wind and gravity—has dominated the uplifted plateau ever since uplift began. Much of the Colorado Plateau has been raised several thousand feet. The Kaibab Limestone, for instance, was once the floor of a shallow sea. Today it forms the rim of the Grand Canyon, 7,000 to 8,000 feet above sea level. Also, the rate of erosion by the Colorado River seems to have accelerated in the past 5 or 6 million years. There is mounting evidence that the rate of down-cutting continues to increase.

What created the canyons? In the past 5 to 6 million years the rate of Colorado Plateau uplift has increased, increasing the down-cutting power of the Colorado River. The river has cut deeply into the high plateau. Gradually, older and older rock units have been revealed in the floors of the canyons. The swiftness of canyon-cutting has been breathtaking, not allowing enough time for the canyons to widen into valleys.

While canyon-deepening is driven by the volume and gradient of the river at the bottom, canyon-widening is controlled by the climate along the canyon rims. Here in the Colorado Plateau, canyon-widening is rather leisurely (because precipitation is minimal) while canyon-deepening is vigorous (because the master river carries relatively large flows from distant, higher, wetter regions down a river corridor of steep gradient).

What led to the formation of Grand Canyon? This is the Colorado Plateau's ultimate geologic enigma. To discover the full story of Grand Canyon's formation, hundreds of geologists would trade in their most treasured rock hammers. Geologists are pretty sure of many parts of the story—the uplift of the Kaibab Plateau, the evolution of drainages on the uplifted plateau, the down-cutting by the Colorado River, the timing and sequence of events. But some parts of the story are completely incompatible with other parts: It can't all be true and there are still some missing pieces to the story.

In general, it seems that the ancestral Colorado River found a shortcut to the sea when the Gulf of California was created about 5 or 6 million years ago. (The gulf formed as the Pacific Plate slid northward relative to the North American Plate along the San Andreas Fault.) The shortcut increased the river's gradient and its erosive power, allowing it to cut fast and deep. Thus the Colorado River, in a relatively short period of time, has been able to cut a deep trench, the Grand Canyon, through a high plateau that (because of its relatively dry climate) has allowed in the same amount of time, surprisingly little canyon widening.

Buckskin Gulch

Slide Arch

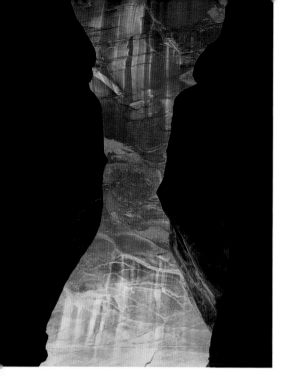
Buckskin Gulch

Just how big is Grand Canyon? It is 277 miles long, averages about 10 miles wide, and reaches just over a mile in depth. The volume of the Grand Canyon (the amount of rock that's missing) comes to about 800 cubic miles. This figure, however, does not include the volume of rock that's been worn away from the landscapes upstream of the canyon and funneled through it to the Gulf of California by the Colorado River. Nor does it include the mile-thick stack of rock that once rested on top of what is now the rim of Grand Canyon. The "missing rock" volume of Grand Canyon is therefore only a small portion of the volume that's been removed by the Colorado River and its predecessors. Still, using the figures of 800 cubic miles of missing rock and 5 million years for the age of the canyon, the Grand Canyon grows bigger by an average of about two-thirds of a cubic foot per second!

Only a few tens of miles of Grand Canyon rims are paralleled by paved road. Many more miles of rim lands are without any kind of road or trail access. Because the rim of Grand Canyon is extremely convoluted (following not only the 277-mile length of the master river canyon but each of a myriad of side canyons) the length of the Grand Canyon's two rims comes to an astonishing 2,750 miles!

It's important to understand that although the Grand Canyon looks very big and very old, it is neither. It looks big because it is unusually deep in comparison to its width. And it looks old because of its untamed demeanor, its size, and the age and character of its rock units.

It's important to understand that although the Grand Canyon looks very big and very old, it is neither.

Why is it that the canyon possesses such a clear-cut rim rather than a muddle of ever higher overlooks, each one still more distant? One striking characteristic of Grand Canyon is its unambiguous rim. Grand Canyon's rim rock, the Kaibab Limestone, is about 260 million years old. Like most of the still older rock units that lie beneath it, the Kaibab is exceedingly resistant to erosion. The younger rock units that once lay on top of the Kaibab were relatively soft and have therefore been carried away by weathering and erosion. It is the definitive contact between the resistant Kaibab and the overlying soft (and now absent) Moenkopi and Chinle formations that gives Grand Canyon its explicit rim.

Most of Glen Canyon, just upstream of Grand Canyon, is walled with those same younger, softer rock units that are missing at Grand Canyon. Because no dramatic "hard rock-soft rock" boundary occurs in the upper levels of the Glen Canyon rock sequence, it has no well-defined rim.

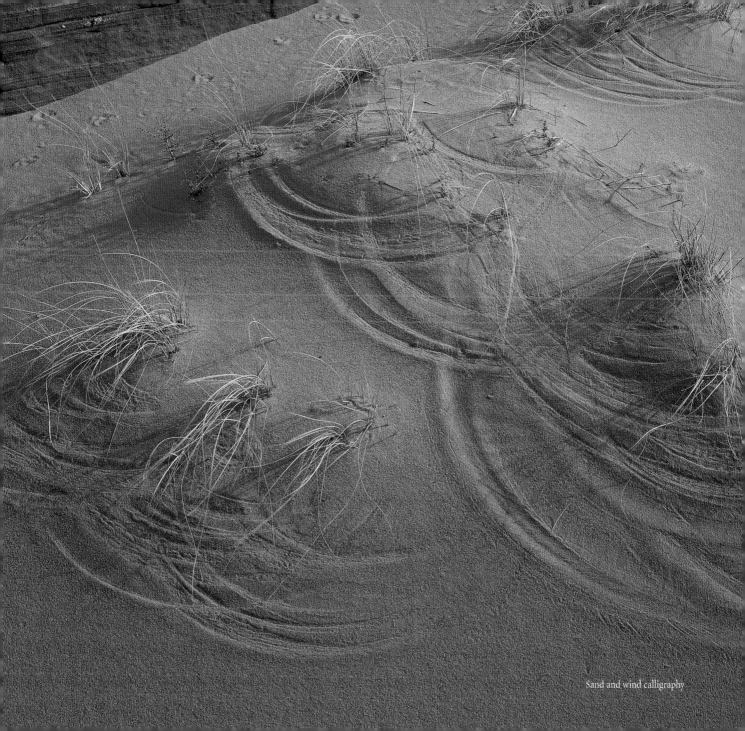

Sand and wind calligraphy

Edge of the Colorado River, river mile 168

Colorado River and Vishnu Group shoreline, river mile 127

Why do some rock units erode into cliffs while others become slopes? In general, the harder a rock unit, the more likely it will weather into a cliff. The softer a rock unit, the more likely it will weather into a slope. The rims of canyons and the tops of mesas develop on the upper surfaces of relatively hard cliff-forming rocks, the overlying soft rock units having been washed away.

Where the opposite situation exists, where soft rock layers underlie resistant rock layers, the rapidly-eroding underlying soft layer undermines the resistant layer above it. Eventually pieces of the resistant layer break off as slabs and blocks which fall, slide and roll down the slope below. The downhill trip usually fragments the rock into still smaller pieces that offer far more surface area to the environment. Having been thus "divided," all the fresh surfaces are attacked by the process of weathering and the rock is easily "conquered" by water, freezing temperatures, wind abrasion and chemical decomposition. After tens, hundreds or thousands of millions of years of existence, the block of fallen rock will rapidly disintegrate in a period of time measured not in millions but in thousands of years.

If a small canyon is cut exceptionally quickly, it becomes a slot canyon. Most slot canyons form because they are carved very quickly as the result of a change in drainage patterns. Most slot canyons of The Hub are usually found in the Navajo Sandstone. The Navajo Sandstone is respectably thick near Page—over 1,100 feet—and considerably thicker in Zion National Park. It's made of windblown quartz sand from a desert that lay here almost 200 million years ago. During its long burial its grains were cemented together by calcium carbonate carried by ground water circulating between the grains.

If a small canyon is cut exceptionally quickly, it becomes a slot canyon.

Today, Navajo Sandstone is a cliff-forming, surprisingly homogeneous, tan-to-orange rock. Although it typically stands straight and tall as a mighty cliff, Navajo Sandstone is no match for flood water soups of sand, silt, pebbles and cobbles. It yields.

Here's a common way in which this can happen: Rockfalls can block established drainage paths. So can windblown sand dunes during a prolonged drought. When the drainage once again runs with water, a new route is sometimes found around, rather than through, the blockage. The bypass canyon can be cut very rapidly because the gradient at the blockage is unusually steep, especially at first when the new canyon just begins to form. The canyon remains especially narrow for hundreds of years because the normal canyon-widening processes are slow to catch up. The sculptured walls of some canyons like Antelope Canyon reflect the swirling flood waters that carved them swiftly and recently.

Navajo Sandstone: contorted bedding

Navajo Sandstone: contorted bedding and erosional sculpture

Are such catastrophes common in geologic history? Is there evidence of great catastrophes in the rock units of the Colorado Plateau? From the human perspective, true, large-scale catastrophes are extremely rare. From the geologic perspective, however, events that we short-lived humans would regard as catastrophes are quite common. Catastrophes come in all sizes, of course, from floods or storms that rage for minutes to hours, to giant meteor impacts, the explosion of nearby supernovas and massive volcanic eruptions that affect the biosphere for hundreds or millions of years.

About 245 million years ago, a few million years after Grand Canyon's Kaibab Limestone was deposited, Earth experienced an environmental disaster of proportions unequaled elsewhere in the geologic record. Geologists call it "The Great Dying." More than 90 percent of Earth's species perished. The origin of the mass extinction is still being debated.

A later extinction event, about 65 million years ago, wiped out not only the dinosaurs but up to 75 percent of Earth's species. This event, we now believe, was caused or exacerbated by the impact of a comet or meteor about six miles in diameter. It struck the Earth near Mexico's Yucatan Peninsula. The energy release is beyond comprehension—equal to that of the detonation of 8 billion Hiroshima-sized atomic bombs.

When catastrophes visit the earth some species will be indifferent to the changes and will simply carry on. Others will be put at disadvantage. Some of those will, in the long run, succeed in coping by evolving into new species that are better adjusted to the altered environment. Others will fail to cope—they will perish.

When large-scale, long-lasting catastrophic changes occur, the Earth itself more or less rolls with the punch. Change is inevitable and Earth responds by transforming into a slightly different planet. It's the planet's life forms that take it on the chin in the transition.

Sand, Lake Powell visitor's sculpture

Hamburger Rocks

Despite the fact that The Hub is surrounded by some of the most interesting landscapes on Earth, despite the fact that much of the area is protected within national parks and monuments, and despite the fact that the area was relatively untouched as recently as 50 years ago, this hallowed ground has suffered grave damage.

The damage came quickly. Within just a few years, the dam was built, the canyon was flooded, roads were paved, a coal-fired power plant was constructed, power lines were sent marching across the plateaus, the air was fouled. Then, out on the new lake, dimwitted boaters carved their names in places almost no one had ever seen before.

Such desecration will increase as more human beings are allowed a home on the planet. We can't have both zillions of people and zillions of acres of unspoiled land. We are converting land, trees, air and plants into human biomass, a high-risk behavior. With so many people making so many demands on our environment, we're just begging for trouble, looking to learn just how far we can go before a "dope slap" is administered by Mother Nature.

The human population grows by about 1 million people *every five days*.

In the long term, the setting aside of natural reserves, national parks and monuments, will not be allowed to stand in the way of the comforts of a human population way out of proportion to its support facilities. We are placing our home in danger. Our world as we know it is in fact so threatened that current efforts to save it are puny in comparison. The situation is so dire that I would almost recommend we just go ahead and ravish the place. We'll get what we deserve. But our children—and our paradise full of interesting plants and animals—would also suffer the consequences.

It's fairly common to assume that the world today is much like the world has always been. Geologists, however, tell us that this could not be further from the truth. The Hub, for example, has been in the not too distant past covered with mountain ranges, oceans, river deltas, swamps, lakes and more. It has been blanketed with volcanic ash and drowned beneath inland seas. It has been shoreline and coastline, desert and dune. It has surely been many things we cannot imagine because no evidence remains.

The canyon country is, at most, a few million years old. In a few million years more, The Hub's paradise will have been erased by erosion if not by more dramatic means. We are but visitors in a temporary phase of an ever-evolving terrain.

As you visit The Hub, remember that many of us live, not like kings, but far better than kings. We have cell phones to communicate with whoever we want whenever we want, cars to zip us around our cities and countryside, aircraft to zip us around the planet, TVs and movies to entertain us, electricity to do our work, the medical establishment to help us live longer and better. We're asking a lot of our old planet. Keep this in mind as you praise the beauty of our unspoiled lands. It is not clear that we can have both all our toys and a refuge like The Hub.

Face Canyon, rippled sands

Entrada Sandstone boulder

Cross-bedding, Navajo Sandstone

Pedestal rock: A conglomerate boulder balances on a siltstone tower

Preposterous landscapes around The Hub

The Hub is surrounded by a cluster of preposterous landscapes. Why have so many wild landscapes developed here? It's because so many flat-lying sedimentary rock units are in various stages of unveiling.

The Colorado River and its tributaries continue to strip away overlying rock to reveal what's been hidden for tens to hundreds of millions (and even billions) of years. The color and texture of the old rock can be ravishing and the shapes of the liberated sediments can be extravagant. This book features a few such terrains, all of them remarkable and all of them nearby:

GLEN CANYON, DOWNSTREAM FROM THE DAM. Each of the 15 miles of Glen Canyon that survived inundation by Lake Powell are jewels. River-runners of the 1940s and 1950s rarely mentioned this reach of river because it was overshadowed by the beauty and drama of the canyons that lay upstream and down. Even so, this short section of Glen Canyon is pure magic with its sheer walls of orange-red sandstone, many cobble bars and secluded glens.

LAKE POWELL. Much could be said about Lake Powell's many high aspirations and its unforgivable mischiefs. Here I'll ignore the debate about which is uppermost to focus on its visual impact. Lake Powell is as rich in beauty and interest as any landscape on earth. Moreover, the lake's fluctuating surface levels re-create the lake every year, swallowing former wonders, revealing and transforming others. Islands, bridges, towers, beaches, cliffs all come and go with the years.

HORSESHOE BEND (TAD NICHOLS OVERLOOK). This viewpoint of the Colorado River at the southern edge of Page takes one's breath away. Many visitors must sit down before they swoon from grandeur…or fear. The symmetry of the canyon's path and the sweep of the river makes Tad Nichols Overlook one of the most photogenic viewpoints in the entire Colorado Plateau.

GRAND CANYON. Grand Canyon, of course, has no equal. Its size, its intricacy and its elemental structural coherence make it one of earth's most sublime landscapes. Meanwhile, down at the bottom of the canyon, the Colorado River continues its work of grinding the canyon deeper still, and carrying out its task with artistry. The shoreline of the Colorado River in Grand Canyon—where the tireless river meets steadfast rock—is a trove of beauty all by itself. It all begins at Lees Ferry at the foot of Glen Canyon.

Cape Royal

VERMILION CLIFFS NATIONAL MONUMENT. This land of sandstone enchantment is more commonly known as northern Arizona's Paria Plateau. It's composed of two worlds, one high, and one low: Paria Canyon has fashioned an underworld where water erosion dominates, sculpting, shaping and staining the canyon floor and walls. In the upper world on the surface of Paria Plateau, wind erosion dominates, shaping the sandstone into domes, hollows, towers, hoodoos and fins.

Rainbow Bridge

RAINBOW BRIDGE. It's a marvel of symmetry carved from Navajo Sandstone, a sculptural masterpiece hidden in the labyrinth of canyons that once came down to the Colorado River before Lake Powell intruded, and a magnet to large numbers of visitors. But without knowing it, pilgrims to this single most obvious wonder of Rainbow Bridge are saluting 10,000 landscape wonders that dwell in the sandstone labyrinths of the Glen Canyon area.

ANTELOPE CANYON. Slot canyons are rather common in the Lake Powell area. Antelope Canyon, however, is the most astonishing and photogenic. Other slots may be deeper, darker, longer and spookier. But none can surpass Antelope's overwhelming photogenic appeal…at least not

without rappelling, swimming and climbing. In Antelope Canyon you can witness the power and beauty of fast-moving water recorded in stone.

GRAND STAIRCASE – ESCALANTE NATIONAL MONUMENT. For sheer variety, complexity and size, this park is unsurpassed. Much of the landscape is open desert but here and there, often hidden below the general land surface in canyons and clefts, are oases of water and refreshment. The frequent discovery of treasures of paleontology keeps this new park in the headlines. Expect to hear more from Utah's Grand Staircase–Escalante National Monument.

Looking down 1,100 feet to the Colorado River

Leaving Balanced Rock Canyon

Testing traction

Double Vision IV: Spider web of fins

Shapes of flowing water recorded in rock

 83

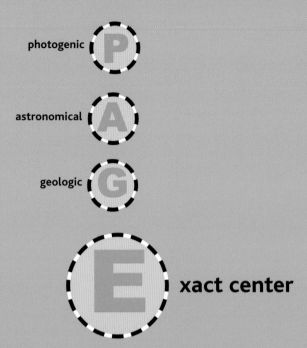

photogenic **P**

astronomical **A**

geologic **G**

E xact center

Yoo Hoo! Anybody else out there?

Because our galaxy is host to at least 400 billion stars and because recent discoveries show us that planets routinely orbit stars, chances seem good that life-friendly planets are numerous. The geologic record of Earth indicates that life appeared here almost as soon as Earth's crust solidified. The same rapid colonization may have occurred elsewhere. Life may be pervasive.

The incidence of intelligent life, however, seems far less likely. Intelligent life requires, if Earth's history is any guide, billions of years of development, even on a planet exceedingly friendly to life and evolution. The vast number of stars in the Milky Way argues that, somewhere, sometime, somehow, other technological civilizations have grown up and flourished in our Milky Way, yet neither do we find convincing proof of contemporary visitation (even in Roswell), nor have we stumbled upon a single petrified extraterrestrial beer can or candy wrapper lost during some ancient visit.

So, where are they? Why haven't they called?

Perhaps the cost of space travel is out of sight, or the vast size and daunting hazards of interstellar space are insurmountable. Perhaps the aliens (traveling without windows to open or refreshing pit stops to anticipate) just can't cope with a decades-long cruise in the confines of a tin spaceship.

The most likely explanation as to why we haven't heard from the neighbors is because advanced civilizations are a short-lived galactic phenomena. Perhaps intelligence and technology are no guarantee of longevity. Perhaps, instead, they are the foundations of self-inflicted, self-limiting disasters. Civilizations may develop the technology to communicate and travel across the galaxy at about the same time that they exhaust their resources, lethally pollute their environment, or fall victim to their own clever gadgets.

Judging from what I see here at home, I wonder if civilizations lose their ability to distinguish between what's important and what's not. They lose their bearings and collapse.

Here's what we do know: Planet Earth is a speck in a very large, exceptionally inhospitable universe. Our speck, to us, is paradise. But we also know our speck of Earth hasn't always been a paradise, and it won't always be one into the future. A supervolcano, a stray comet, a rogue asteroid, or a lethal load of large scale rotten luck of any kind will end it. We know that time is running out. We know this because time always runs out. Sooner or later forces beyond control will strip us of our good fortune.

Given this larger perspective it becomes obvious that our earlier definition of The Hub is too confined. The entire planet—oceans, mountains, rivers, deserts, plains, glaciers, swamps, cocoon of air and myriad forms of life—is The True Hub. As far as we know, there is not another like it in all the universe.

If the history of Earth were compressed into a three hour movie, our part, the part that our species participates in, would last the entire final second. We haven't been here long, but we're having a spectacular, largely detrimental effect. Perhaps we're just following the customary, unavoidable trajectory of all planetary civilizations—a fortuitous birth, a lengthy period of stumbling progress, a short-lived crescendo of sensational achievement, then rapid decline brought about by 'irrational exuberance.'

Meanwhile, until we get lucky or smart, let's appreciate our day in the sun. Personally, I'm humbled by the whole pageant of cosmic history, the burned out stars that cooked up the heavy elements that make life possible, the condensation of our solar system from a cloud of gas and dust, the earth's 4.6-billion-year maturation, the evolution of life towards ever more sophisticated forms, the rise of humankind, and the hundreds of thousands of human inventors, scientists and explorers that have made us exceedingly wealthy and surprisingly knowledgeable. It's quite a story.

FINAL EXAM: PAGE, AZ.—HUB OF THE UNIVERSE

1) *Which is oldest?*

   p) Grand Canyon

   a) Vishnu Schist

   g) Navajo Sandstone

   e) The phrase "Have a nice day."

2) *Dinosaurs never roamed the Grand Canyon. Why not?*

   p) Dinosaurs flourished, then fell into extinction long before the canyon was carved

   a) The canyon's terrain was far too rugged for the lumbering beasts

   g) The National Park Service thought their presence would jeopardize visitor safety

   e) The canyon's climate was too hot and dry for such large animals

3) *Why should Hub photographers avoid slot canyons in wet weather?*

   p) Clouds are detrimental to most slot canyon photographs

   a) Cameras and (especially) lenses, pointing upwards, will get wet and sandy

   g) Visitors and their cameras can be washed away by sudden, horrific flashfloods

   e) All of the above

4) *Why is the South Rim lower in elevation than the North Rim?*

   p) The Kaibab Plateau in the area of Grand Canyon gently tilts down to the south

   a) The top three layers of rock on the South Rim were shaved off by glaciers

   g) Heavy visitation on the South Rim

   e) Extreme subsidence caused by overly ambitious extraction of uranium ore from South Rim's Orphan Mine

5) *In 1994 we Earthlings saw what happens when the highly improbable occurs on a cosmic scale. What did we see?*

   p) Aerial surveillance of O.J. Simpson cruising the L. A. freeways in his Bronco

   a) A cow carefully tip-toeing across an area of fragile sandstone fins and cross-bedding features

   g) Several impact sites on Jupiter where of a series of large comet fragments smashed into the planet

   e) Both p) and g)

6) *Colorado River flows fluctuate from hour to hour in Grand Canyon. Why?*

   p) Synchronous boat launchings on Lake Powell

   a) Wild changes in the low humidity desert evaporation rates of the Colorado River—morning, high noon, evening and midnight

   g) Dam overflows caused by today's super-sized Lake Powell swimmers

   e) Fluctuations in power demand, environmental considerations and other factors

Answers: 1-a), 2-p), 3-e), 4-p), 5-e), 6-e)

Quicksand!

Before . . .

. . . and only moments later.

"Listen; we are here on Earth to fart around.

Don't let anybody tell you any different!"

Kurt Vonnegut, *Timequake*